# WATCHMAN NEE

# Burden and Prayer

**Living Stream Ministry**
Anaheim, CA • www.lsm.org

© 1993 Living Stream Ministry

All rights reserved. No part of this work may be reproduced or transmitted in any form or by any means—graphic, electronic, or mechanical, including photocopying, recording, or information storage and retrieval systems—without written permission from the publisher.

ISBN 978-1-57593-868-4

*Living Stream Ministry*

2431 W. La Palma Ave. Anaheim, CA 92801
P. O. Box 2121, Anaheim, CA 92814 USA

15  16  17  18  /  8  7  6  5  4

# BURDEN AND PRAYER

Scripture Reading: Jer. 33:2-3; 1 Thes. 5:19

### ONE

Every child of God should have some God-given burden. No child of God can say that God has never given him or her a burden. However, burdens can only be received from God when our spirits are open to Him. An open spirit to God is the condition for receiving burdens from God. Having received a burden, we must learn to discharge it faithfully through prayer. When we have discharged the first burden, we will receive a second, and when the second is discharged, we will receive a third. Therefore, the most important thing is to open our spirits to God. We should say to God, "I open myself before You to pray." Because of our unfaithfulness we often do not receive any burdens; therefore, if we want to be those who bear God's burdens, we must be very sensitive and not reject any feeling that comes from Him.

If we feel we should pray for something, we should do it immediately. At the outset, these feelings may be faint, but they will gain in strength as we go on. If we quench the Spirit and do not release our burden through prayer, we will lose our burden. Then the only way to recover it is to confess our sin and thereafter faithfully respond to every God-given feeling. As soon as we are moved to pray, we should pray. As we faithfully discharge the burdens we have, God will continually give us further burdens to bear. The sole reason for not receiving further burdens is that we have not released the burden we already have, and the unreleased burden has squelched us. If we unload the burden, a second burden will follow. A burden may be very faint at the beginning, but we must be faithful to it. If we are faithful to do this repeatedly before the Lord, God will continue to dispense burdens to us one after another. O brothers and sisters, if we hope to be of any use to God, we must recover our lost burdens.

Burdens are especially related to the work of God. Therefore, we must seek to do His will in everything and wait on Him in His work until He communicates His burden to us. His burden is the manifestation of His will. The burden we receive is the very will of God, and it is also the means by which God manifests His will.

For example, God may give you a clear and strong burden to preach the gospel. If you go along with it and act according to God's will, the more you preach, the more the burden will be released. The burden may be heavy at the beginning, but the more you preach, the lighter the burden will become. However, if you fail to discharge your burden, it will weigh down heavily on your spirit, and you will feel its weight becoming heavier and heavier as time goes on. Eventually, your feeling will become numb, and you will no longer feel the burden. The life within will seem to perish, and there will seem to be a barrier between you and God. (This does not mean that you will eternally perish, as in the case of eternal perdition; it merely means that you will feel as if your life has ceased.) It will seem as if you can no longer touch God and that the burden has crushed you. All spiritual work issues from such burdens. If you try to work without a burden, your work will be ineffective. But if you work in accordance with the burden that is upon you, your whole being will be increasingly liberated as you advance. You may start off by having a heavy burden, but as you go on, the burden will be released, and you will be uplifted. The value of your work depends on the burden you bear in connection with it. Without a burden, there is no spiritual value to your work. But with a burden, there is spiritual value. Every time you work according to a burden, you will be refreshed and edified. As your load is discharged, you will be edified in the process. If you work without a burden, you will sense that you are laboring in vain and may even be conscious of reproof as you labor. In relation to all spiritual work, you should wait on God for His burden and then set out to discharge it in a conscientious way.

## TWO

But this does not mean that we need to constantly look within to discover whether or not we have a burden. Among God's children, there is nothing more damaging than introspection. Let us bear this in mind—the most damaging thing is to turn our gaze inward. This may be even more serious than sin. Sin is readily recognized as such, but introspection is not detected so easily. An unsuspected disease is always more serious and damaging than an apparent one. If you were asked whether it is wrong to be proud, you would immediately answer that it is obviously wrong. If you were asked whether it is wrong to be envious, you would know quite well that it is wrong. These flaws are obvious. But you can become introspective twenty times in a single day without any sense of wrongdoing. If you quarrel, you soon become aware that you have done something wrong; you quickly identify your sickness. But you can be introspective and be totally unaware of its evil. Looking within is the most hurtful thing in the Christian life. Many Christians are given to introspection, and they are living a life of false spirituality. Before doing any work, they stop and ask, "Do I have a burden for this? Is the feeling I have a burden or not? Is this a burden? What is a burden?" If a man continually asks these questions, he does not know what a burden is.

Suppose someone asks you to help him carry a table from one room to another. While you are doing it, do you wonder whether this is a burden? Would you say that it is not a burden if it were lighter and that it is a burden if it were heavier? No. As long as something is burdening you, it is a burden. Remember that a burden is what you know, not what you have to discover. If you have a burden, you know it. It is wrong to look inward to see whether or not you have a burden. A burden is known rather than found. It is of great importance to recognize this fact. There is no profit in introspection. The greatest damage a Christian can suffer comes from introspection; it will cheat you. It is not necessary to look for a burden day and night. If you feel that you should preach the gospel to someone and you stop to ask whether or not you have a burden, the opportunity will disappear while you are asking your questions. O brothers and sisters, it is unprofitable to look within. Whether or not you have a burden will be apparent—either you have a burden or you do not. In both cases you will know; there is no need to discover one. If you have to turn inward to find one, you do not have a burden. There is no need to ask anything. If you have it, you will know. If anything weighs upon you, that is your burden.

If you feel heavy within, you have a burden, and if you act in accordance with it, you will be liberated. Then you will be free to receive further burdens from God, and you will be edified in the process. All the work of God is done this way. The ministry of prayer is carried on this way. Prayer and work are inseparable. Without prayer, there is no work. Therefore, you have to learn to pick up burdens as well as release burdens through prayer. The Lord may put a certain matter within you and give you a burden for it. If you pray, it will be released, and you will be refreshed. But if you do not pray, you will be crushed beneath the burden. If you do not pray today, tomorrow, or the next day, you will feel bothered whenever you think about it, and the burden will become heavier and heavier because you have not done what you are supposed to do. After setting it aside once or twice, eventually, you will not feel it anymore. If you repeatedly act contrary to your feeling, at a certain point you will not feel it anymore. You will lose touch with God and no longer be able to fellowship with Him. A barrier will develop between you and God because you have betrayed the burden and not acted according to God's direction. Every work has to be conducted with a burden, whether the work is directed toward God or toward men. At the same time, once you have a burden, you should act according to the burden. If you do not act according to the burden, you will become deadened because you have violated God's will. A burden is a necessary requirement in God's work. Once you have a burden you have to work accordingly.

### THREE

While it is true that the burdens we have are from God and that our burden is God's will, it is also true that our knowledge mainly governs our burdens initially. There are exceptions. For instance, God may call certain things to our remembrance and may ask us to pray for them, or in the middle of the night God may call us to get up and pray for a brother in a remote place. These experiences do occur, but they are not common, and God does not do this kind of thing very often. Sometimes God cannot find anyone nearby, and He has to go to someone far away; however, these are exceptions. Under ordinary circumstances, God directs men according to their knowledge. This is why we say that knowledge governs a burden in its initial stage. However, after one has knowledge, it does not necessarily mean that he will have a burden. We may know about the condition and everything else related to certain brothers and sisters yet not have any feeling for them or be stirred up within. We have the knowledge, but we do not have the burden. Therefore, burden does not come ultimately from knowledge. Yet knowledge does govern our burden in its initial stage. For example, God may give you knowledge of certain matters and the burden to pray and help out the situation. In this way, the burden comes. A burden can be formed at the beginning through knowledge. Most burdens even have knowledge as their starting point. It is rare for God to start a burden without giving any knowledge of it. There are exceptions. Sometimes God may give you a burden to pray for a brother. He may be sick or he may be in difficulty, but you know nothing about it; you have not received any news from him. Yet God puts a clear burden within you to pray for him. Perhaps after a few weeks or a few months, you may receive a letter from him and find that he was indeed sick and in difficulty. There are cases like this, but they are exceptions. They may happen once in a thousand times. Generally, burdens start from knowledge. Yet this does not mean that knowledge is burden.

## FOUR

Since prayer is a Christian ministry and an important ministry, a question arises: When there is a heavy burden to pray, do we express it through words, or should we be quiet and silent? Can we just bear our burdens silently before God?

We believe that if God gives us a prayer burden, then He wants it to be uttered. If we have only a few disjointed words, we should express ourselves with these words. Burdens are released only through utterance. If we remain silent before God, the burden will not leave; rather, it will become heavier and heavier upon you. Brothers and sisters, in the spiritual realm, it is an amazing principle that utterance counts. God takes account not only of what we believe but also of what we say. He is mindful not only of the intents of our heart but also of the words in our mouth. Our Lord said to the Canaanite woman,

"Because of this word, go. The demon has gone out of your daughter" (Mark 7:29). The few words the woman uttered caused the Lord to work. We may make a request in our hearts, but there is more effect in an uttered request. God seems to require that we speak what is in our heart. The Lord's prayer in the Garden of Gethsemane was a crucial prayer, but it was a prayer with "strong crying" (Heb. 5:7). We do not insist on loud prayers. Sometimes there is no need to pray in a loud way. But if there is a heavy burden within, there should be a correspondence between the inner burden and the outward expression. If the burden within is not strong, loud prayers are nothing but noise. But if the burden within is heavy, it must be uttered with audible sounds. If we cannot pray aloud in our homes, let us find a place where we can utter our burden as the Lord did. At times He went to a deserted place (Mark 1:35) and at other times He went to the mountain (Luke 6:12). Even if we cannot go to the wilderness or the mountain, we should pray audibly even if it means praying in a low voice. The important thing is that our prayers have to be audible. If our burden is strong enough, we can find a suitable place to pray. God wants our burdens to be articulated. If we have not articulated our burden, the burden will remain. Some say that they pray silently and that it matters little whether or not the burden is released. This is not true. If a man has not finished the work he has in his hands, he cannot go on to more work. In the same way, if our burden is not released, God cannot give us another burden. We have to discharge our burden with our words so that God can give us a fresh burden.

But very often our difficulty is that even when we are conscious of a burden to pray, we do not know how to pray when we kneel down. We know that something is weighing within us, but we do not know how to pray. There is a burden in our spirit, but we do not know what to pray. We need to realize that our burden is a matter of the spirit, whereas our comprehension of the burden is a matter of the mind. When our spirit touches our mind, we will understand the nature of the burden in our spirit. When the spirit and the mind touch, both will become clear. Some people feel that they have a burden but do not know what it is. This is because their spirit has not yet touched their mind.

Therefore, when their spirit has a burden, their mind does not comprehend the burden. How can contact between the spirit and the mind be established? It is quite simple. If you want to find anything, how should you go about it? If it is to the west and you go east, how would you find it? You would have to circle the globe before you found it. The object may be only a mile away, but you would have walked around the globe before you found it. You should take the point where you are as the center and look around in a circle, moving out steadily from the center to the circumference, expanding the circle as you move. In this way, you can cover all four directions. This is the best way to look for things. When your spirit has lost touch with your mind, you should do the same thing. When you kneel down to pray, do not hold on tenaciously to one thing. That would be like walking in one direction, and you will not find what you are looking for easily. Pray for many things and from many directions. After praying a few sentences for one thing, you may feel that it is not the right thing to pray about. You should drop it and change to another subject. You may have to change your subject two, three, or four times. Or you may become clear after you come to the second subject. You may also have to mention five or six things before you feel that you have touched something that releases your burden; once you pray for this, your mind and your spirit become linked together. You should then pray specifically for that matter in order to release your burden. Once you pray this way, you will feel released, and when you have released your first burden, you will be ready to receive a second burden from God.

## FIVE

Many Christians cannot be used by God in the prayer ministry because they are over-burdened. They have never released any of their burdens. God gives them a burden to pray, and they may know what it is; their mind and their spirit may be connected, yet they do not pray. Instead, they allow the burden to become heavier and heavier until they are so crushed that they cannot bear it any longer; the feeling for the burden will be gone, and they can no longer pray. Oh, brothers and sisters, the work of God will be seriously hampered if we do not have a free spirit to serve as instruments for His use. If we asked someone to help us with a certain job but found that his hands were full, it would be useless to seek his aid. In the same way, if we are weighed down by many burdens, how can God commit anything further to us? This is why we must release our burdens. The release of the burden will set us free, and God will be free to give us additional burdens. Without this, we will not be able to fulfill a ministry of prayer before the Lord. The ministry of prayer requires a liberated spirit. If we have a burden in our spirit and do not pray for it, we cannot go on to a second thing. If we have a burden but are not faithful to pray and take up the ministry of prayer before the Lord, we will feel heavy the first day, heavier the second day, and still heavier the third day. After a few more days, the burden will gradually go away, and the strength to pray will be gone as well. If we have a burden and do not pray, eventually it will cost us our prayer ministry. We must, therefore, devote time to fulfill our ministry of prayer. The best way to pray is to pray with two or more people; this will save us from being individualistic. Many people have not learned to pray together with others. In praying with others, we must not only pray with our mouths but listen with our ears. If we learn to pray in this way, the "spiral" prayer that we mentioned earlier, praying from the center to the circumference, will come into effect. Through prayer, we can release the burden that God has given us. Prayer frees our spirit and liberates our being. This will allow God to commit fresh burdens to us continually. Today God needs the cooperation of His church on the earth, and we can cooperate with Him through prayer. May there be a way for the working out of His will!